D0777078

Created and published by Knock Knock
1635-B Electric Avenue
Venice, CA 90291
knockknockstuff.com

Illustrations by Gemma Correll

ISBN: 978-160106487-5
UPC: 825703-50015-8

100 Reasons to Panic about Having a Baby

KNOCK KNOCK®
VENICE, CALIFORNIA

1.

You can't even keep a plant alive—how will you take care of a baby?*

*Plants don't cry when
they're hungry; babies do.

2.

Privacy will become a foreign concept. So will freedom.*

*Yes, but you won't be lonely
(no matter how much you'd like to be).

3.

You'll think your kid is hideous when it pops out.*

*If you'd spent nine months cooped up in the same place, you wouldn't look so hot yourself. It'll get cuter.

4.

You won't bond with your newborn.*

*You'll be together 24/7; with that much togetherness you could bond with a rock.

5.

You'll never have time to read anymore.*

*You'll get to enjoy classics such as
How to Use This Rectal Thermometer and
the back of the Children's Tylenol box.

7.

You'll never sleep again.*

*That lack-of-sleep fog is just like being drunk without the pesky hangover.

8.

Once you're a mom, you'll wear mom jeans.*

*The high elastic waist means
you can eat whatever you want.

9.

Once you're a dad, you'll wear dad jeans.*

*Dad jeans are better than bad genes.

10.

Non-parent friends won't want to hang out with you anymore—because you're boring.*

*They'll die sad and alone.

12.

You might
bonk the baby's
head on a
doorframe.*

*You will do this at least once.
Don't worry: see Reason 11.

13.

Your parents and in-laws will be overbearing with their advice.*

*Your mutual desire to kill them will bring you and your partner closer.

14.

Dinner out
means a 5:00 P.M.
reservation at a
"family-friendly"
restaurant.*

*Anything's better than cooking it yourself.
You can also qualify for the early-bird special.

15.

Your house will never be clean.*

*Studies show that environmental dirt actually strengthens your baby's immune system.

16.

You'll yell at your kid.*

*If you don't, how will she learn to deal with mean bosses and coaches in the future?

18.

You're having a girl.*

*Now you can read someone's diary!

19.

You're having twins. Or—eek—triplets.*

*At least your kids
will always have a playmate.

20.

You won't be able to stop swearing, damn it.*

*There's nothing funnier
than a toddler with a potty mouth.

21.

You can't hit the bars anymore.*

*Drinking at home is cheaper.

23.

The name you thought was so unique will rocket to popularity.*

*When you go to amusement parks, she'll always be able to find a personalized key chain and mug.

24.

The name you thought was so special is actually just plain weird.*

*At least he'll always be able to get an email address with his name in it.

25.

You'll stop traveling to fantastic, faraway destinations.*

*You'll still get all the fun of packing—
it will just be for a day at the park, and will
require more than a carry-on's worth of stuff.

26.

You'll start driving a kid-friendly car like a station wagon, or worse, the dreaded minivan.*

*Not worrying about spills and paint scratches is seriously liberating.

27.

Your kid will never shut up.*

*You'll tune out two-thirds of what she says.

28.

You're too young to have a kid.*

*By the time your kid is out of
the house, you'll just be hitting your prime.

29.

You're too old to have a kid.*

*You'll enjoy awkward moments with strangers while they wonder if you're the haggard mom—or the hot granny.

30.

You'll never save enough to send your kid to college—no matter how many fancy lattes you forgo.*

*Join the club.

31.

You'll become an unemployable has-been with no professional relevance.*

*You can start a parenting blog and turn it into a bestseller. Some successful bloggers are making up to seven figures a year.

33.

You'll have to sit through insipid kids' movies.*

*This is how you'll catch up on your sleep.

34.

One day,
your precious
baby will rebel
and cover himself
in tattoos.*

*You'll be the person behind the
"Mom" (or "Pop") inked on his chest.

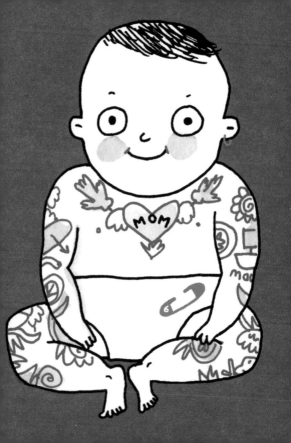

35.

You'll gain
a boatload
of pregnancy
weight.*

*Oh, please.
There's a whole other person inside there.

36.

Your kid will be traumatized by daycare.*

*Those teachers will probably be way more creative and patient than you. If you're really lucky, they'll potty train your kid, too.

38.

Your wardrobe budget is sure to shrink, if not disappear.*

*Baby clothes are really cute.

39.

People without children will think your kid is a spoiled brat.*

*They're just empty-hearted and bitter.

40.

Even the most compatible couples start to fight once they have a kid.*

*Dinner + couples therapy = date night.

41.

You'll never wear cashmere or silk again.*

*You'll save on dry cleaning.

42.

You'll have to
answer your
kid's questions
about sex.*

*Better he learns it
from you than on the streets.

44.

Toys will overtake your life—and your living room.*

*That Barbie Dream House
you always coveted can now be yours.

45.

Baby poop will make you puke.*

*That's nothing that two days with a newborn won't solve.

46.

You'll have to endure endless games, matches, meets, and practices.*

*You're bound to find at least one kindred spirit among all those annoying parents in the stands.

47.

Your baby boy will pee all over you.*

*You'll develop astonishingly
quick reflexes, and these reflexes will come
in handy for so many other needs.

48.

You'll hunger for adult conversations.*

*You'll be able to tell a stegosaurus (spiked tail) from a triceratops (bony frill behind head).

49.

You won't be able to change a diaper.*

*Have you ever assembled anything from IKEA?
You'll be able to change a diaper.

50.

Baby weight
is hard to lose.*

*Pediatricians say breastfeeding
can burn 500 or more calories a day.
Not breastfeeding? See Reason 66.

51.

Your kid will be
a terribly picky
eater.*

*More food for you.

52.

Your kid will have crazy food allergies.*

*Some people pay good money
to be on gluten and dairy-free diets.

53.

You'll ruin your kid by allowing her to watch too much TV.*

*The average child watches three
to four hours of TV a day.
Shouldn't your kid be above average?

54.

You have a dog and, frankly, you never trained him well. How will you rear an actual child?*

*Everyone knows a dog, as well as your firstborn, is just a practice run.

55.

You'll dread changing your baby's diapers and fantasize about letting her sit in it.*

*If you're lucky,
someday she'll change yours.

56.

You'll want to go back to work and you'll feel guilty.*

*You'll get to leave the house!

58.

After the whole birthing experience, your partner won't look at you the same way.*

*For a brief moment, you'll see each other as godlike beings. After that, you'll both be too tired to notice each other at all.

59.

Your kid will be a biter and chomp on other people's children.*

*What better way to weed the hypervigilant parents out of your life?

61.

You'll never have sex again.*

*You'll get quick and stealthy,
like a nookie ninja.

62.

You'll be that person who constantly shows photos of his kid to strangers.*

*You'll have an excuse to buy a fancy new camera.

63.

You'll be obsessed with reading product labels and making sure everything is nontoxic.*

*Baby's first word will be "polyethylene terephthalate," a sure sign of genius.

64.

Alone time—
what's that?*

*Going to the bathroom by yourself
will feel more luxurious than a day at the spa.

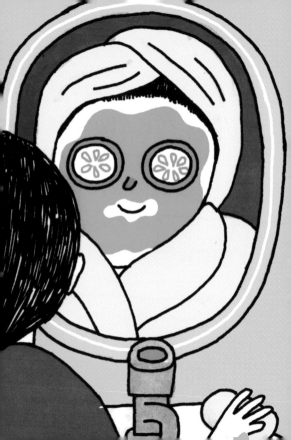

65.

The kid will ruin your nice furniture and break stuff, like that pricey vintage vase you got at an Italian flea market.*

*You'll get to practice
the Zen art of impermanence.

66.

You won't have time to exercise or go to the gym.*

*Have you ever seen a toddler go?
You'll get nothing but exercise.

67.

Strangers like to fondle a pregnant belly.*

*It's great prep for eighteen years of having your personal space invaded.

68.

You'll have to participate in dozens of Play-Doh and Lego sessions.*

*You'll find your inner child;
it's in there somewhere.

69.

All the toddler fits, meltdowns, and tantrums will drive you to drink.*

*You'll be well prepared for adolescence.

70.

Your teenager will hate you.*

*She will, and then she won't, and then she will, and then she won't, and then it will be the next day and you'll start all over again.

71.

Going out to eat will be a nightmare.*

*You'll be amazed at
how speedy the service will be.

72.

You'll have to help
your kid with
math homework.*

*Maybe this time you'll get it.

73.

Your spouse will be a lousy parent.*

*If it doesn't work out,
at least you'll have the kid.

74.

You'll invite scorn when you give up on cloth diapers and switch to disposables.*

*Having a child increases your average lifetime carbon footprint by nearly six times, so it's sort of pointless worrying about cloth vs. disposables at all.

75.

Date nights will become a thing of yore.*

*Think of all the money you'll save on sushi, for Pete's sake. (Did someone say sake?)

76.

You'll lose track of your toddler in a crowded public place.*

*They usually only go far enough to give you a mild coronary.

77.

Your kid will be a conservative.*

*You can embarrass him at rallies.

78.

Your kid will be a liberal.*

*You can embarrass her at rallies.

79.

Sometimes your baby looks kind of creepy, like a miniature old man.*

*It's unlikely you'll be around when he's eighty, so it's your window into the future.

80.

That food fight you narrowly escaped in high school is now mealtime at your house.*

*Scrubbing the floor tones your biceps and can burn up to 400 calories an hour.

81.

You'll have to childproof everything.*

*That's impossible. Unless you have a giant plastic bubble. And the giant plastic bubble is probably a suffocation risk.

82.

Your kid
will be bullied.*

*Discovering your inner mama
(or papa) bear is empowering.

84.

Your beloved pet won't like the baby.*

*When the kid starts dropping food on the floor they will become best friends.

85.

Your kid will ask questions like "Why is the sky blue?" and other countless classics you can't answer.*

*You will actually learn that the sky is blue because the wavelengths of blue light passing through particles in the air are the right length to be most visible.

86.

You'll slip up on the Santa secret.*

*There are undoubtedly worse secrets you could let slip.

87.

She'll cry
and you won't know
what's wrong.*

*You won't have a clue what's wrong.
But you'll figure out the wet cry, the tired cry,
and the hungry cry—eventually. Then you'll
feel like the baby whisperer.

88.

You'll raise the school troublemaker.*

*You'll develop really tight relationships with the principal and teachers.

89.

Puberty will kill you.*

*You survived it once, you'll survive it again;
this time you won't have zits.

90.

You won't like your kid's friends.*

*Some days you'll like
his friends more than you like him.

91.

You'll be the parent on the airplane with the screaming baby.*

*It will distract you from your fear of crashing.

92.

You won't think your kid is cute (aka "What if he gets Grandpa's nose?").*

*You're biologically preprogrammed to think they're cute. This is what keeps you from selling them.

93.

The baby will bite while nursing.*

*Only once: babies don't like it when you shriek and fling them from their food source.

94.

You'll become just like those parents you used to mock.*

*If you do, you probably won't realize it.

95.

You'll feel guilty at work all day long.*

*You'll feel guilty about everything as a parent.
At least this one comes with a paycheck.

96.

You'll constantly compare your kid to others, and worry that he's not meeting milestones on time.*

*Those babies who walk at six months will disappoint their parents in plenty of other ways later.

98.

You'll never be cool again.*

*Your kid will think you're totally cool.
Until middle school.

99.

You'll become just like your parents.*

*Well, you turned out okay—
in spite of all the mistakes those idiots made.

100.

You'll screw your kid up, utterly and completely.*

*You'll either keep her future therapist employed—or be a major part of her memoir.

* Don't worry.
It's worth it.